DRAWING
PRINCESSES, TROLLS,
AND OTHER FAIRY-TALE CHARACTERS
An Augmented Reading Drawing Experience

BY CLARA CELLA

ILLUSTRATED BY LISA K. WEBER

CAPSTONE PRESS
a capstone imprint

Dabble Lab Books are published by Capstone Press,
1710 Roe Crest Drive, North Mankato, Minnesota 56003
www.mycapstone.com

Library of Congress Cataloging-in-Publication data is available
on the Library of Congress website.
ISBN: 978-1-5435-3190-9 (library binding)
ISBN: 978-1-5435-4237-0 (eBook PDF)

Summary: This drawing guide is playful, pretty, and popping with princesses
and other characters straight out of a storybook. Step-by-step instructions show
readers how to draw fairy-tale subjects that increase in difficulty to strengthen skills
and confidence. Readers can download the Capstone 4D app for an augmented reality
experience that extends learning beyond the printed page with artist video tutorials
and other bonus content.

Editorial Credits
Jill Kalz, editor; Aruna Rangarajan, designer;
Kathy McColley, production specialist

Photo Credits
Capstone Studio: Karon Dubke, 31 (pop-up castle); Shutterstock: Bimbim (flower
background), cover and throughout, Jamen Percy, 5 (pencils and scribbles), Lifestyle
Graphic (sheet of paper), cover and throughout, Mega Pixel, 5 (erasers and pencil
sharpener), Ruslan Ivantsov, 5 (graphite pencil), timquo, 5 (felt marker)

Printed in the United States of America.
PA017

TABLE OF CONTENTS

HELLO, ARTIST!

You never know whom (or what) you'll meet in a fairy tale. A kind princess? A fearless prince? Maybe a beastly troll living under a bridge? You're about to meet *all* of these folks, plus six more. They've come from faraway, make-believe lands to have their portraits drawn by you. (A castle's ready for its close-up too.)

Warm up with the easier projects toward the front of the book. Tougher projects are toward the back. Follow the step-by-step instructions, and practice, practice, practice. If you need help, scan the star targets. Your 4D drawing instructor will magically appear, ready to help—

POOF!

—just like a fairy godmother!

Tools and Supplies

Before you begin your drawing projects,
gather the following tools and supplies:

PAPER
Any type of blank, unlined paper will do.

PENCILS
Pencils are the easiest to use.
Make sure you have plenty of them.

SHARPENER
You'll need clean lines, so keep
a pencil sharpener close by.

ERASER
Pencil erasers wear out very quickly.
Get a rubber or kneaded eraser.

DARK PEN/MARKER
When your drawing is finished, you can
trace over it with a black ink pen or a thin
felt-tip marker. The dark lines will really
make your work pop.

COLORED PENCILS
If you decide to color your drawings,
colored pencils usually work best.

CASTLE

No fairy tale would be complete without a castle. With their stone walls and tall towers, castles are usually home to kings and queens. But all sorts of fairy-tale characters, including witches, can live in them too. If a castle is enchanted, a spell (good or bad) has been cast upon it.

STEP 1

STEP 2

STEP 3

STEP 4

Does your castle sit atop a snowy mountain or a grassy hill? Does it lie beneath the sea? Draw the surrounding area.

STEP 5

PRINCESS

Fairy-tale princesses can come in all shapes, sizes, and colors. They're not always human, either! For example, Hans Christian Anderson's little mermaid is part human, part fish. She's the daughter of the Sea King. And Princess Fiona, from the modern-day fairy tale "Shrek," is a creature called an ogress.

STEP 1

STEP 2

STEP 3

STEP 4

Once you've drawn your princess, add a pattern to her dress. Try flowers, stars, or swirls.

STEP 5

EVIL QUEEN

What's one thing all fairy-tale evil queens want? Power! They also want to be the most beautiful woman in the land. They lie, use magic, and sometimes harm others to get what they want. Two of the most famous evil queens appear in the stories "Snow White" and "Sleeping Beauty."

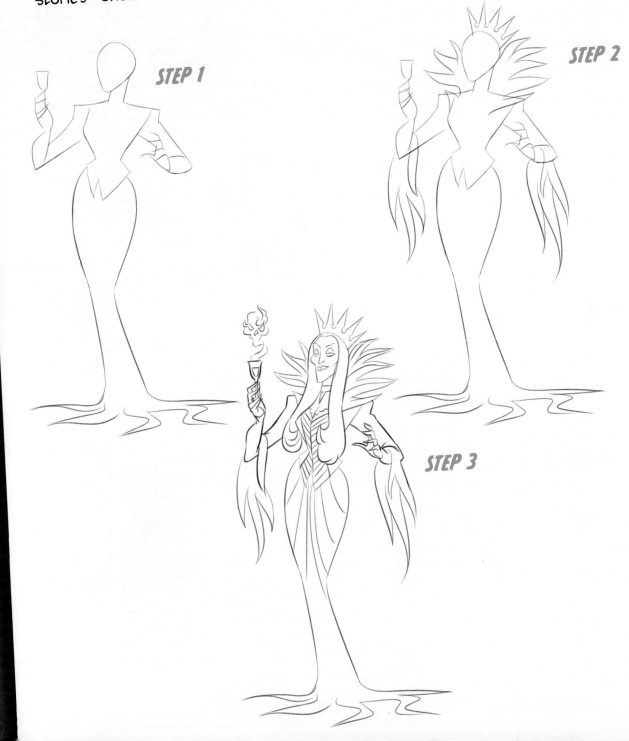

STEP 1

STEP 2

STEP 3

STEP 4

STEP 5

Anyone who drinks this evil queen's potion will turn into a toad. Draw a bunch of toads at her feet.

Fairy godmothers are imaginary beings who use magical powers to keep people safe and happy. With a flick of her wand, the fairy godmother in "Cinderella" turns rags into a beautiful gown. She turns a pumpkin into a carriage, mice into horses, and a rat into a coachman.

STEP 1

STEP 2

STEP 3

STEP 4

After you've drawn your fairy godmother, try drawing her again. This time, add bigger, fancier wings.

STEP 5

MERMAID

Don't challenge a mermaid to a swimming contest. Or a sing-off. You will lose both! Part human, part fish, mermaids have powerful tails that help them glide through the ocean. Their lovely singing voices have enchanted sailors around the world for thousands of years.

STEP 1

STEP 2

STEP 3

Draw a few underwater friends for your mermaid. Try some fish or a sea turtle. Maybe an octopus.

STEP 4

STEP 5

OGRE

In traditional fairy tales, ogres (OH-gurz) are big and ugly. And they stink. Oh, and they eat people. They aren't the kind-hearted creatures you know from today's stories, like Shrek. Some of them have magical powers too. The ogre in "Puss in Boots" can change himself into any animal—from an elephant to a mouse.

STEP 1

STEP 2

STEP 3

STEP 4

STEP 5

After drawing
your ogre, try
drawing his wife.
A female ogre is
called an ogress.

TRICKSTER

Tricksters pop up in fairy tales all around the world. They play clever tricks to fool others out of their riches. Tricksters take many forms. Common animal tricksters include foxes, wolves, monkeys, rabbits, and spiders. One of the best-known tricksters? An odd little man named Rumpelstiltskin.

STEP 1

STEP 2

STEP 3

STEP 4

Once you've drawn your fox trickster, try drawing a sneaky partner for him. Maybe a monkey or a rabbit.

STEP 5

The witch smiles a sickly smile. Her bird looks like it knows a secret. Beware! Don't make the same mistake Hansel and Gretel made when the witch in their story offered treats. *Just say no.* Or you may wind up on the dinner menu!

STEP 1

STEP 2

STEP 3

STEP 4

STEP 5

Fairy-tale witches love magical spells and potions. Try drawing a large pot of bubbling potion for your witch.

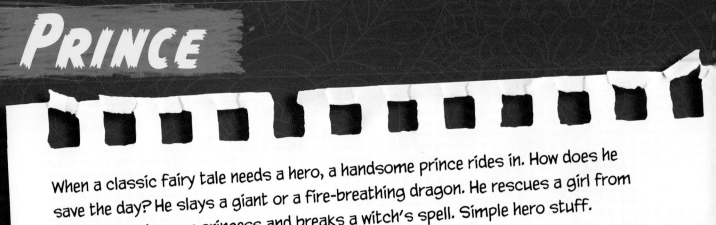

PRINCE

When a classic fairy tale needs a hero, a handsome prince rides in. How does he save the day? He slays a giant or a fire-breathing dragon. He rescues a girl from a tower. He kisses a princess and breaks a witch's spell. Simple hero stuff.

STEP 1

STEP 2

STEP 3

STEP 4

CONTINUED...

STEP 5

STEP 6

Not all heroes look alike. Draw the horse again. But this time, draw the hero *you* want to see riding it.

STEP 7

STEP 1

Think twice before crossing this ugly troll's bridge. He's mean and ready to gobble up anything in sight! Trolls first appeared in fairy tales from Norway and Sweden. In some of those stories, trolls came out only at night. If sunlight hit them, they turned into stone.

STEP 2

STEP 3

STEP 4

CONTINUED...

STEP 5

Try drawing the goats from the fairy tale "The Three Billy Goats Gruff" on top of the bridge.

STEP 6

CRAFT IT UP!

AND THEY LIVED HAPPILY EVER AFTER . . . But wait! This book doesn't end here. Pick your favorite drawing and craft it up!

POP-UP CARD

WHAT YOU NEED:

- two pieces of colored cardstock (one 5.5 x 8.5 inches [14 x 22 cm] and one 5 x 8 inches [13 x 20 cm])
- a pencil
- white cardstock
- scissors
- a ruler
- an adult
- a craft knife
- clear tape
- glue

STEP 1 Fold both pieces of colored cardstock in half so the short ends meet. The larger piece is the outside of your card, and the smaller piece is the inside.

STEP 2 Draw the fairy-tale image you picked on the white cardstock, twice.

STEP 3 Cut out your images. Leave one 0.5-inch (1.3-cm) tab at the bottom of each image.

STEP 4 Have an adult help you make two slits in your inside piece of colored cardstock with the craft knife. Each slit should be about 0.5 inches on either side of the fold, centered, and long enough for your tabs to fit through.

STEP 5 Insert the tab of one of your images into a slit. Flip the card over and tape the tab in place. Repeat this step with your second image. Make sure both images are facing the same way.

STEP 6 Set the inside piece on top of the outside piece. Match the folds. Then glue together. Next glue the tops of both images together. Let dry.

STEP 7 After the glue has dried, gently close the card, then open it again to see the magic!

STEP 8 Add glitter, jewels, or other items to make your card sparkle.

Don't forget to write something and sign your name.

READ MORE

Disney Storybook Artists. *Learn to Draw Disney's Classic Fairy Tales: Featuring Cinderella, Snow White, Belle, and All Your Favorite Fairy Tale Characters!* Forest, Calif.: Walter Foster Jr., 2018.

Masiello, Ralph. *Ralph Masiello's Fairy Drawing Book.* Watertown, Mass.: Charlesbridge, 2013.

Sautter, A.J. *How to Draw Elves, Dwarves, and Other Magical Folk.* Drawing Fantasy Creatures. North Mankato, Minn.: Capstone Press, 2016.

INTERNET SITES

Use FactHound to find Internet sites related to this book:

Visit *www.facthound.com*

Just type in 9781543531909 and go.

MAKERSPACE TIPS

Download tips and tricks for using this book and others in a library makerspace.

Visit *www.capstonepub.com/dabblelabresources*